About the WOMEN OF OUR TIME® Series

Today more than ever, children need role models whose lives can give them the inspiration and guidance to cope with a changing world. *WOMEN OF OUR TIME*, a series of biographies focusing on the lives of twentieth-century women, is the first such series designed specifically for the 7–11 age group. International in scope, these biographies cover a wide range of personalities—from historical figures to today's headliners—in such diverse fields as politics, the arts and sciences, athletics, and entertainment. Outstanding authors and illustrators present their subjects in a vividly anecdotal style, emphasizing the childhood and youth of each woman. More than a history lesson, the *WOMEN OF OUR TIME* books offer carefully documented life stories that will inform, entertain, and inspire the young people of our time.

"Taking its cue from Burnett's apparently boundless optimism, Howe's biography is cheerfully upbeat.... While clearly relishing the fairytale aspects of Burnett's rise to fame, Howe does not disregard the pain in the comedienne's life (and its contribution to her talents). Recommended."

—Bulletin of the Center for Children's Books

CAROL BURNETT
THE SOUND OF LAUGHTER

BY JAMES HOWE
Illustrated by Robert Masheris

PUFFIN BOOKS

To my parents,
who shared the laughter—
and passed the popcorn

J.H.

PUFFIN BOOKS

Published by the Penguin Group

Viking Penguin Inc., 40 West 23rd Street, New York, New York 10010, U.S.A.

Penguin Books Ltd, 27 Wrights Lane, London W8 5TZ, England

Penguin Books Australia Ltd, Ringwood, Victoria, Australia

Penguin Books Canada Ltd, 2801 John Street, Markham, Ontario, Canada L3R 1B4

Penguin Books (N.Z.) Ltd, 182–190 Wairau Road, Auckland 10, New Zealand

Penguin Books Ltd, Registered Offices: Harmondsworth, Middlesex, England

First published in the United States of America by Viking Penguin Inc., 1987

Published in Puffin Books 1988

1 3 5 7 9 10 8 6 4 2

Text copyright © James Howe, 1987

Illustrations copyright © Robert Masheris, 1987

All rights reserved

WOMEN OF OUR TIME® is a registered trademark of Viking Penguin Inc.

Library of Congress catalog card number: 88–42962

ISBN 0-14-032075-X

JPB 92-196

Printed in the United States of America by R.R. Donnelley & Sons Company, Harrisonburg, Virginia

Set in Garamond #3

CONTENTS

1

The Little Mermaid

Once upon a time there lived a skinny little girl with straight brown hair and scratched-up knees. Her name was Carol Burnett. She got the knees from roller-skating, but she was never quite sure where she got the hair. Looking in the mirror over the bathroom sink, she'd scowl at what she saw: that stringy mop, those big front teeth, and a chin that almost wasn't! She couldn't help thinking of her good-looking mama and daddy and wondering why she wasn't pretty.

But then she'd settle into the tub for a good, long soak and forget what she'd seen in the mirror. The only sounds in the room were the ticking of the clock and the soft lapping of water as she swished it to and fro. Soon she was far off in another world, an underwater world of mystery and magic. She imagined herself to be the Little Mermaid, one of her favorite fairy-tale characters. And for an hour or two, she was beautiful.

Beyond her bathroom door, away from her dreams, was the messy one-room apartment she shared with her grandmother, whom she called Nanny. Down the hall was her mother's apartment. And outside was Hollywood.

Hollywood, California, at the beginning of the 1940s, when Carol was growing up there, was America's "dream factory." It was a time when Americans badly needed to dream. About to enter a world war, the American people looked to the movies for laughter and for hope. And Hollywood was where the movies were made. The movie stars were like kings and queens who acted out fairy tales for ordinary people—grown-ups as well as children—to believe in.

Carol hadn't been born in Hollywood, but she'd come close to being born at the movies. If her mother had stayed to watch the end of *Rasputin and the Empress,* she might well have been. But Louise Creighton Burnett wisely rushed from the San Antonio, Texas, theater where the movie was playing and got to a hospital in time. Carol was born on April 26, 1933.

Carol's father, Joseph Thomas Burnett, who was called Jody, had been the manager at the movie theater where *Rasputin and the Empress* played, but that job, like most of the others he tried his hand at, didn't last long. Tall, handsome, green-eyed Jody was a charming man, but he had a serious illness that made it impossible for him to hold on to jobs—or anything else. He was an alcoholic.

In 1935, when Carol was two, her parents moved to California to find work and give themselves a fresh start. Carol was left in Texas to be raised by Nanny. Lou, as her mother was known, wrote to Nanny and Carol of her hopes of getting a job as a writer. Jody wrote of his battles with drinking, and he urged his young daughter to pray for him. These letters made Carol feel guilty because even when she prayed, her father kept on drinking.

In time, Lou was drinking as heavily as Jody. And their marriage was falling apart.

Carol didn't know much about her parents' lives at that time. They lived a world away, and her world was taken up with dolls and roller-skating and going to the movies. Nanny loved the movies, too, so it is not surprising that Carol's earliest memory is of watching a movie at age four.

When she was seven, Carol took a long train trip

with Nanny to California. She didn't recognize the pretty woman who ran to meet them at the other end. The woman picked Carol up and kissed her. She kissed Nanny, too, and seemed excited to see them both. Carol wasn't excited so much as she was tired and confused.

As she and Nanny picked up their suitcases and followed the woman out of the train station, it suddenly dawned on her who this stranger was. "Mama," she thought. "It's Mama."

Lou, who was no longer living with Carol's father, had found Carol and Nanny an apartment down the hall from hers so that the family could be closer together. When they arrived, Lou unlocked the door and handed the key to Nanny. Carol wiped the tiredness from her eyes and gazed at the place she would call home for the next fourteen years.

Apartment 102 faced the lobby. It was tiny, with one bed that pulled down from the wall and no closets. Carol hung her clothes on the shower rack in the bathroom, and though the skirts and blouses changed over the years, her "closet" didn't. Her clothes were always damp.

Life wasn't easy in her new home. Nanny and Mama fought all the time. And when things got to be too much for her, Nanny just closed her eyes and threatened to die. This terrified Carol, who depended on her grandmother for everything. It made her feel she could never let Nanny out of her sight. "I thought she was going to drop dead if I wasn't taking care of her, or watching after her," she told an interviewer once. "If Nanny went, that would be the world blowing up."

But Nanny didn't die. She might not always have shown it, but she loved Carol as much as Carol loved her. And she was determined to give her the best care that was possible on the welfare check that came from the government once a month.

Being on welfare meant, in Carol's own words, "that we were poor, and that once in a while I'd get some clothes that had been worn by other little girls, and they'd be in a grocery bag."

Carol and her grandmother used empty jelly jars for glasses and stole sheets of toilet paper from public bathrooms in order to save money. But the rent was paid. And there was always enough money left over for the movies. Carol put it best when she said about going to the movies with Nanny, "That was our life." Getting there before the prices changed at six o'clock, they paid as little as eleven cents and saw as many as eight movies a week.

Since they lived only a block away from Hollywood Boulevard, it wasn't difficult for them to go to the movies that often. The street was lined with theaters.

Several nights a week, it was lined with fans as well. At that time in Hollywood, when a movie opened, it was a big event. The stars came to the openings wearing long gowns or tuxedos.

This was the Hollywood of dreams, just a few streets away from the other Hollywood, the one Carol described as "a real neighborhood, where we roller-skated and played ball in the street and sold lemonade on the corner." In the Hollywood of dreams, mothers and grandmothers didn't scream at each other. Families didn't have to drink out of jelly jars and steal toilet paper. And ugly ducklings always turned into beautiful swans.

2

Who Shall I Be?

Carol's favorite actress as a child was Linda Darnell, who was everything Carol wished she could be—self-assured, silky-haired, and glamorous.

One night, when Carol was nine or ten, she was standing by Nanny's side behind the rope that separated the fans from the stars. Suddenly she spotted Linda Darnell. Her heart stopped. "Linda, Linda!" she heard her grandmother call out. "Now, this little girl just worships you! Why don't you give her your autograph?"

Carol watched in disbelief as the actress walked

straight to her. Her heart was beating quickly now, rising up into her throat, making it hard to breathe. "That's very nice," the actress said, bending down to smile at Carol, "and I'm very flattered. What's your name?"

Carol opened her mouth, but nothing came out. Her throat was filled with the beating of her heart, her nose with the smell of perfume, her eyes with the sight of a face even more beautiful than the Little Mermaid's. And then Carol noticed something: "I saw that her nostrils weren't the same size."

Of course, no one's nostrils are exactly the same. But to Carol this came as a surprise. Beauty wasn't perfect. Even so, she decided, Linda Darnell *was.*

When she wasn't going to the movies or watching for movie stars, Carol liked to play with her friends. Her best friends were Ilomay and her cousin Janice, whom she called Cuz. One of their favorite games was jacks. But what she liked best, either alone or with her friends, was pretending to be someone else.

"My friends and I used to go to the movies whenever we possibly could," Carol said. "When the movies were over, we'd go . . . up a hill . . . until we came to our private place. Then we would replay the movies we'd seen."

When she played with Cuz, who was prettier, Carol took the men's parts. (One of those parts was Tarzan, and to this day no one does the "Tarzan yell" better than Carol Burnett!) But when she played with Ilomay, who let her be the boss, Carol was the pretty one.

And when she was alone in Apartment 102, she pretended to be a one-person radio show.

She'd raise the window that opened onto the neighbors' apartments, and shout out an entire show featuring herself as both announcer and guest singer. One day a man yelled, "Turn that radio off!" She was thrilled. Her act had been convincing.

She was also thrilled the time she convinced her friend Asher that she was her own twin sister, Karen. Switching clothes and dashing in and out of her apartment through every available door and window, she held Asher spellbound in the lobby. First she was Carol; then she was Karen, who spoke with a British accent and squealed with delight at being reunited with her long-lost twin. She kept the routine going for six days until she was worn out and Asher began to catch on.

As much as Carol liked to pretend, however, it never occurred to her that she might be an actress one day. Pretending was something she did for fun— or to make herself feel better when her mother and grandmother fought. Besides, actresses were beautiful. She wasn't. Her mother often reminded her

that she wasn't likely to make it in the "looks department," so she'd better plan on working at something where looks didn't matter.

Her grandmother had her own ideas for Carol: Go to secretarial school, get a job, and grab the boss. Nanny firmly believed that if a woman wanted power, she had to marry a powerful man.

Carol wasn't sure what she wanted to do. She loved to draw, and she was good at it, so for a long time she thought she'd be a cartoonist. In high school, she considered sports. At fifteen, she was able to outrun all the boys in the hundred-yard dash. But despite her ability as an athlete, she felt more awkward and self-conscious about her appearance than ever. Remembering herself as a teenager, she joked, "I was so desperate not to be noticed that people would come over to where I was sitting and ask, 'Is this chair taken?' "

She no longer dreamed of being the Little Mermaid. It was easier to be invisible. Her half sister, Chrissy, born in 1944, when Carol was eleven, had a natural beauty Carol knew she'd never possess. It was foolish to want what she couldn't have. But what did she want? What could she have?

The only area her mother had encouraged her in was writing. "Stick to journalism," she had told her. "No matter what you look like, you can always write."

Working on the newspapers at Le Conte Junior High School and Hollywood High had given her a way to be noticed without having to be seen. And she did like to write.

Carol's thoughts turned from fairy tales to reality. She was not going to settle for her mother's life of empty dreams and empty bottles, or her grandmother's plans of secretarial school and marrying the boss. She wanted something better for herself. She would become a journalist—a newspaper and magazine writer—and she would go to college to learn her craft. She set her sights on attending the University of California at Los Angeles (UCLA), a college nearby. But in some ways, that desire felt like a bigger dream than wishing to be the Little Mermaid.

After all, tuition was forty-two dollars, more than their monthly rent! There was no way she could afford it. But in her mind's eye, Carol *saw* herself at UCLA. She just knew she had to go there.

Then one morning something of a miracle happened.

She found an envelope in her mailbox with her name written on it. Inside was a fifty-dollar bill. There was no note, and she never found out who had left it for her. All she knew was that for the first time in her life, her dreams were coming true.

3

The Sound of Laughter

Carol enrolled at UCLA after graduating from Hollywood High School in the winter of 1951. Much to her surprise, the university offered no course in journalism. In trying to decide what to study instead, she was drawn over and over to the pages in the college catalog describing the theater arts program. It was true that theater arts offered a course in writing plays, but she knew it wasn't the writing that attracted her. No, it was the growing awareness that what she really wanted was to be an actress.

An actress? Her?

Crazy.

But then she remembered all those movies she'd acted out with Ilomay and Cuz and her other friends, the times she'd shouted and sung her radio show from the open window of Apartment 102, those six days she'd actually made Asher believe she was her own twin sister, Karen. She thought about singing harmony with Mama and Nanny in the kitchen, imagining them to be the three Andrews Sisters, a popular singing group of the time. She saw herself dancing and dreaming and pretending. And she knew: these were the times she felt most alive, not when she was writing. As she would put it later, "I came to life the times I wasn't me."

So she enrolled in the theater arts program.

She didn't tell her mother or grandmother of her decision. She was much too worried they wouldn't approve. Besides, being a theater arts student meant she would have to perform—in front of other people.

Acting 2A was a required course for everyone in the theater program. Because Carol was late in joining the class, the other students had already been paired up to present scenes. She would have to perform a speech by herself. Her part was that of Irma, a waitress who, while clearing a table, talks to the audience of her love of beauty and her desire to be loved.

It never occurred to Carol to read the whole play, in order to make sense of the scene. She simply learned the words of her part and, a few days later, rattled them off in a dazed monotone that could barely be heard. Her arm moved awkwardly back and forth in an attempt to pantomime a waitress wiping a table. The class, not sure *what* to make of her performance, misunderstood and thought she was supposed to be ironing. She received a D minus.

The next time she acted in a scene, she had only two words to say, but they happened to be funny words. Everybody laughed. She stuck to comedies for the rest of the term and wound up with an A minus in the course.

It wasn't long before she dared to perform for more than the handful of students in Acting 2A. Soon she was cast in a one-act comedy open to the entire school. In the play, called *Keep Me a Woman Grown,* she had the part of Effie, a hillbilly woman. In preparing for the role, she remembered the people she'd known as a little girl in Texas. That helped give her the character's way of speaking. And she used her expressive face and voice to get the laughs.

And what laughs she got! When she returned to the stage for her second scene and uttered her line, "I'm back," the audience wouldn't let her go on speaking. They laughed and clapped and stomped their feet. And Carol stood there feeling something she'd never felt before. It was happiness. No, it was *bliss.*

"The first time I forgot I was homely," she recalled later, "was the first time I heard an audience laugh."

Suddenly Carol Burnett was no longer invisible. She wasn't even trying to be. Her performance as Effie received a glowing review in the school newspaper. And she was asked to try out for some scenes to be put on by the music department. Carol had always loved to sing, but only for herself. Her mother had a sweet voice and perfect pitch. When she thought of her own voice, the only word that came to mind was "loud." Still, she had dared a lot already. Why not dare a little more?

Now, when she sang in front of other people, she did what she had always done. She pretended to be somebody else—she played a part. The songs were funny, and the audiences laughed, and her confidence grew.

Over time, she wanted to share this part of her life with her family. So she invited them to a performance of one of the programs put on by the music department. By the time the lights dimmed and the show was ready to start, she was a nervous wreck. Would her family tell her what she'd feared such a short time ago—that she was crazy to want to be an actress?

When it was all over and she saw her little sister, Chrissy, run to her with open arms, when she heard

Nanny introducing herself to everyone as "Carol Burnett's grandmother," when she saw the look in her mother's eyes, she knew it was all right.

"You really were the best one," her mother told her.

And she was. At the end of her first year, she won the theater arts department award for most promising newcomer.

Promise gave way to fulfillment as Carol acted in many more productions over the next few years. She was invited to join a talented group of UCLA graduates at their summer theater near San Francisco. And she added something new to her life: a boyfriend.

For the first time, Carol knew what it was to be in love. A fellow theater arts student, Don Saroyan, was several years older than she. Neither wanted to rush into marriage, despite Nanny's pressures that her granddaughter "get the ring." Their careers were what mattered most at this time in their lives, and nothing was going to stand in their way.

As her third year of college drew to a close, Carol had serious doubts that she would stay and finish her fourth and final year. She and Don had talked about their future; they knew what they wanted: New York.

Just as she had "seen" herself at UCLA, she now saw herself acting and singing on the Broadway stage.

But New York was thousands of miles and hundreds of dollars away.

Once again, a miracle happened.

It happened this time at a party. She and Don, along with other theater students, had been invited to act and sing for faculty members and their guests. After they'd performed, they were approached by a businessman in his fifties.

"I like you two kids," he told them. "What are your plans?"

They replied that they wanted to go to New York but didn't have the money. "What's money?" the man asked. "When I came to this country, I didn't have a cent. Today I'm worth millions. I'll send you to New York. Come see me next week. I'll arrange it."

Don and Carol looked at each other in surprise.

A week later, they called his office. "Be here tomorrow morning at ten," he told them. And when they appeared at the appointed hour, he presented each of them with a check for one thousand dollars.

"There are conditions," he said. "This is a loan. There will be no interest, but I want you to pay it back in five years. You mustn't reveal my name. If you do, everybody will beat on my door. You must use this money to get to New York. And if you succeed in your profession, I want you to help others financially the way I'm helping you."

Carol stared at the check in her hand, which represented more money than she'd ever seen in her life. This was the second time the generosity of a stranger had made her dreams come true.

How could she not believe in fairy tales?

4

A Princess in New York

Carol had never really gotten to know her father when she was growing up. A sweet, gentle man who became sweeter when he drank, he came around from time to time to visit his ex-wife and daughter even after Lou had given birth to Chrissy. If it bothered him that Lou wasn't married to Chrissy's father, he never said so. All he wanted was to see what was left of the only family he had. But Nanny let him in the door only when he had a few dollars to give them. And since a few dollars were hard to come by and harder to hold on to, he hadn't visited often.

Now Carol was leaving California and she wanted to say good-bye. She found her father in the charity ward of a hospital. He was skinnier than she'd ever seen him, sicker than he'd ever been. In his battle with alcohol, the bottle was winning.

But he was pleased to see his daughter and impressed by her plans. "You scared?" he asked her.

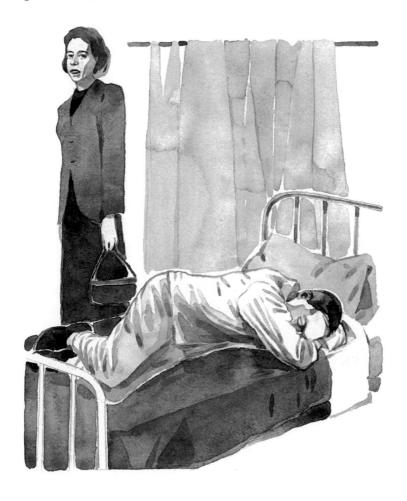

"No. Yeah. A little."

"That's okay," he said. "You any good?"

"I think so." She showed him her college reviews.

"Well, you must be pretty darn good to have all those nice things written about you," he told her.

Carol held his bony hand in hers until it was time for her to go. "Now remember, Punkin," he said, using his pet name for her, "when you get to Broadway, you better get me a ticket to opening night."

"I promise, Daddy," she said. And she started to leave.

She turned back one more time before going out the door. But her father didn't see her. He had rolled over in bed, thinking no longer of Carol but of his own sickness and pain.

Back home, Chrissy was mad at Carol for leaving. Mama was silent. And Nanny told her if she wasn't a star by Christmas, she'd just better come back home. In August 1954 she left for New York.

Because Don was going to follow some months later, Carol found herself alone in a strange city, alone— really *alone* for the first time in her life. She spent her first night crying. The next morning, she wiped her eyes, blew her nose, and set out from the hotel room she couldn't afford to find a place to live.

She found it at the Rehearsal Club.

Home for about fifty young women who were trying

for careers in show business, the Rehearsal Club was a four-story brownstone building on West Fifty-third Street in Manhattan. For eighteen dollars a week, a young actress could share a bedroom and have all her meals.

Since acting jobs were hard to come by, Carol worked at a restaurant, checking hats, to pay for her room and meals. In time, Don joined her in New York.

"Pounding the pavement" is an expression used by actors who are trying to find work. What it means is that the only way to get a job is to go out and walk from one door to another—producers' doors, directors' doors, agents' doors—any door that will open a crack and offer a chance. Carol did a lot of pounding the pavement her first months in New York, but no doors opened—not even a crack. When one finally did, it belonged to an agent who told her to let him know when she was in a show and he'd come see her. How was she going to do that, she asked, when she couldn't get an agent to help her get into a show?

Put on a show yourself, he advised her.

And that's just what she did.

Don agreed to direct the twenty-three Rehearsal Club residents who would make up the cast of the First Annual Rehearsal Club Revue. Each woman pitched in twenty-five cents a night to pay for a place to rehearse. The theater itself, located next to Carnegie Hall, was more costly—over three hundred dollars for three nights. They worked hard and raised the money to make it all happen. But it was worth it.

On March 3, 1955, they opened the first of three sold-out performances. The audience was filled with agents and producers. The young actresses were a hit and, as she had been at UCLA, Carol was the biggest hit of them all.

"Easily the winner . . . was Carol Burnett," proclaimed the newspaper *Show Business* in its review. The reviewer went on to say, "She can sing and pantomime with the best of them, her sense of timing is top notch."

As a result of her stand-out performance, Carol got an agent. (An agent is someone who helps actors find jobs and often takes care of the business side of their careers.) It wasn't long before she had work as well.

Like most other children in the 1930s and 1940s, Carol hadn't grown up with television. In 1945, when she was thirteen, there were more than 56 million radio sets in American homes and fewer than 150,000 television sets. Just ten years later, in 1955, over 35 million TV sets were in use. TV was on the rise, and Carol's star would rise with it.

On December 17, 1955, Carol made her first national television appearance, singing love songs to a puppet on "The Paul Winchell Show." When she called her grandmother to tell her the good news, Nanny asked her to say hello on TV. Carol patiently explained that it would be impossible for her to blurt out "Hello, Nanny!" on national television. When Nanny refused to be convinced, Carol came up with a solution: a secret signal. She would pull her left earlobe, and that would let Nanny know she was all right. Nanny was delighted, and Carol pulled her earlobe at the end of every "Paul Winchell Show" in which she appeared. Or *almost* every show. The one time she forgot, she got a collect call from California asking what was wrong. She never forgot again.

December 17 was an important day in Carol's life for another, more personal reason: she and Don were married. Much to Nanny's satisfaction, Carol had "gotten the ring." But she hadn't had to marry the boss to do it.

While Don struggled to build an acting and directing career, Carol topped one success with another. "The Paul Winchell Show" was followed in 1956 by "Stanley," a weekly TV series. And then in the fall of 1956, she tried out for "The Garry Moore Show."

Between 1950 and 1964, Garry Moore's daytime and nighttime television shows were among the most popular variety programs on TV. To try out for him was a great opportunity.

After she finished her seven-minute piece, Garry

Moore asked her, "Do you have anything else?"

"No, sir," she said. "That's it."

She expected him to say, "Well, come back when you have something else we can see." She was stunned to hear instead, "Okay, I want you on my show."

She wouldn't become a regular weekly performer on "The Garry Moore Show" for another three years, but she was a frequent guest, and her appearances there led to other important programs. On one of these programs, "The Jack Paar Show," she performed a comedy-song number that won her a great deal of attention. The gossip columnists loved it. And the State Department of the United States called the Paar show to request a repeat performance.

Why all the fuss? The song was called "I Made a Fool of Myself over John Foster Dulles." And John Foster Dulles was Secretary of State at the time. Besides the fact that he was an important government official, he wasn't the sort of person anyone was likely to have a crush on. One newspaper writer had gone so far as to label him a "pickle puss." The idea of a love song to John Foster Dulles made people laugh. And no one laughed harder, it was said, than the Secretary of State himself.

Toward the end of 1957, at the height of the "John Foster Dulles" craze, Carol went to California to visit her family. She was shocked by what she found. Twelve-year-old Chrissy was wearing makeup that made her look years older. Mama had retreated to a near-constant drunken stupor in a darkened apartment that smelled of stale tobacco. Nanny, getting older, was having a harder and harder time coping with her daughter and younger granddaughter. Carol spent sleepless nights wondering what to do.

And then it came to her. She would "kidnap" Chrissy.

She could see no other way, even if it seemed a somewhat crazy idea at the time. Here she was, a twenty-five-year-old woman, married only three years, just starting her career. How could she possibly manage to be sister and mother to a teenager? But how could she leave Chrissy in the same kind of messed-up home she herself had escaped years earlier?

Lou saw the wisdom in her daughter's idea and sadly agreed. They kept the plan to themselves, however, because they knew Nanny and Chrissy would not agree to it. Carol invited her little sister to spend the Christmas vacation with her in New York, and Chrissy happily accepted.

On December 11, the day before Chrissy's thirteenth birthday, she and Carol said good-bye to Mama and Nanny. Carol kissed her mother and whispered, "Thank you, Mama. It'll be okay." Carol may have been scared at that moment, but deep down she knew she was doing the right thing.

Christmas 1957 came and went. When Chrissy learned she was not going back home, she lashed out angrily at Carol. But Carol's promises to get braces for Chrissy's teeth and send her to a good private school calmed her down. A few nights later, Chrissy had a dream about Mama and woke with an urgent need to write and tell her how much she loved her.

It was one of the last letters Lou received. She died of alcohol-related causes in January 1958, less than a month after Carol's visit and Chrissy's "kidnapping." She was forty-six.

It was a sad ending to a sad life. But Carol would always remember the good times. "She was very beautiful and one of the funniest, brightest ladies when she was well," she told an interviewer years later. "I miss her very much."

She went to California in March to move her grandmother out of Apartment 102 into a larger apartment nearby. How strange it all was. After all the years Nanny had taken care of her, now she was taking care of Nanny. And soon Apartment 102 would belong to somebody else, somebody she didn't even know.

The next day she returned to New York to get on with her life.

One of Carol's biggest breaks came a year and a half later when she was cast in *Once Upon a Mattress,* a musical comedy version of one of her favorite Hans Christian Andersen fairy tales from childhood, "The

Princess and the Pea." The play would be directed by George Abbott, one of Broadway's top directors. Carol had dreamed of being directed by Abbott. Now another dream was coming true.

The part of Princess Winnifred the Woebegone (called "Fred," for short) fit her talents like a glove. When the show opened on May 11, 1959, an announcement went out to newspapers, stating that its star was a "San Antonio, Texas, beauty" named Carol Burnett. And when the lights went down and the curtain went up that night, the theater was filled with beauty—the beauty of laughter.

The play itself received mixed notices, but critics had only raves for Carol.

Calling the show a fairy tale, one reviewer wrote: "George Abbott enriched the ranks of comics last night. His contribution was Carol Burnett. Miss Burnett has large eyes and [a] larger mouth, a limber body and even more limber vocal equipment. [She] is the funny find of the season."

The audiences loved Carol even more than the critics did, laughing and cheering her on at each performance. She had made it. She was a star.

5

Roses and Thorns

Jody Burnett never got to see his daughter's opening night on Broadway. He had died four years earlier. Abused by a lifetime of very heavy drinking, his body had simply given up. He was the same age as Carol's mother when he died: forty-six.

"My parents had their problems," Carol said, "but they loved me. A lot of kids, whose parents don't drink and who have money, don't have that."

Now the love in Carol's life would come from her audiences and, closer to home, her sister, Chrissy. Carol and Don, however, were growing apart. In March 1960, they decided to separate.

"What made it particularly rough was that Don wanted to be an actor too," she told an interviewer in 1961. "The fact that I was making more dough than Don didn't bother me, but since he was a man it bothered him. One day we just looked at each other and said, 'This is it.' "

She was now a regular performer on the Tuesday night "Garry Moore Show." Her zany acting and spirited singing brought her to a place even stardom on the Broadway stage couldn't: the homes of millions of American television viewers.

Carol's style of comedy was like a refreshing slap in the face to the American people. Here was a woman who seemed to know no bounds, who broke the rules. The 1950s and early 1960s were a time when people didn't speak out, when being like everyone else seemed terribly important. Carol came along and shattered the polite silence. She poked fun at the world, and she started by poking fun at herself.

She still felt unattractive, and she made herself even more so by crossing her eyes and twisting her features into exaggerated masks. "I think when I went into comedy," she once said, "I decided to hit myself first before anyone else did."

"Carol is really an attractive girl, but she thinks of herself as an ugly duckling," Garry Moore once said.

But Carol's thinking was different. "Most

women . . . are afraid that being funny is unfeminine," she said. "There's all that training you've had since you were three. Be a lady! Don't yell or try to be funny! Just be a nice little girl."

Interviewers repeatedly expressed surprise at how pretty Carol was in person. A fan expressed it most directly when she told Carol, "You aren't half as ugly in person as you are on TV."

There's a word for crossing your eyes, twisting your face up, and sticking out your tongue—all for laughs. It's "mugging." Mugging was a popular style of comedy then, and Carol was the best there was at it. Mugging, letting her voice crack, falling down—all of these got laughs, but they did something else, too. They made people feel as if they knew her. Here was a star who wasn't a distant queen, the way movie stars had been when Carol was growing up. She was to many people, simply, "one of us."

"I love you fourth best," one teenage fan wrote her. "First I love God, second my mother, third my nephew, then you."

In no time, Carol was being referred to as "the new first lady of television." She had replaced Lucille Ball (of "I Love Lucy" fame) as the nation's favorite comic actress. In the three years she appeared on the Moore program, she was seen by 24 million viewers each week. Her last year on the show, she won her first

Emmy Award, television's highest honor.

Carol had long since paid back the mystery businessman in California who had made it possible for her to come to New York. She'd sent him a check for one thousand dollars on June 22, 1959, five years to the day he had given her the money. She had opened on Broadway with her dream director and received glowing reviews. She was not only a part of the Garry Moore team, she was one of the most loved performers on television. "Kid," Garry told her, "you can do anything." And it seemed that she could.

After a time, what she wanted to do was move on. In the summer of 1962, she left "The Garry Moore Show," with Garry's blessing, agreeing to come back for some guest appearances. She took with her a wealth of experience and the status of star.

One of Carol's first efforts after leaving Garry Moore was a TV special with Julie Andrews, a big musical comedy star. "Julie and Carol at Carnegie Hall" went on the air on June 11, 1962. It was the first production under Carol's ten-year million-dollar contract with the CBS network. A mix of comedy and song, it was a huge commercial and critical success.

For Carol, it was a personal success as well. She sang a song on the show called "Meantime." It was a ballad, a serious song, and she sang it seriously. She didn't play anyone else and she didn't mug. She was herself, and the audience liked her.

The good things in her life were now coming her way in bunches, like roses from an admirer. But some of the roses had thorns, and they hurt.

Carol had worked closely with Joe Hamilton, one of Garry Moore's producers, for three years, and their friendship had blossomed into romance. Both were separated from their spouses at the time. When they divorced, they married each other.

In 1963, divorce was not as common as it is now. When Carol and Joe married, they had to put up with a lot of unkind gossip. Joe was the father of eight children, a fact that would get much attention in the press. One newspaper reporter was told that Joe's family was against his marriage to Carol, and that they would never accept her.

Over time, Carol was accepted by Joe's family, however. And some of his eight children lived with Joe and Carol on and off in the coming years. On one occasion, Carol fried up sixty-seven pieces of chicken for a single meal! She was happy being Mrs. Joe Hamilton, happier than she had been with Don. Joe wasn't struggling with a career the way Don had been; he was every bit as successful in his work as she was in hers. Besides, he was a decision maker, and Carol said she liked having someone else make the decisions for her for a change.

Still, it was hard knowing that some people didn't approve of her marriage to Joe. She threw herself into her work, and in time the gossiping quieted down.

Another thorn in Carol's bouquet of roses at the time, though a less prickly one, was her first movie appearance. One reviewer said of her performance in the 1963 comedy *Who's Been Sleeping in My Bed?* that it was not "fair to be critical of Carol Burnett, who is making her debut in the movies with a hopelessly foolish role." Carol's own review was even more direct. "I didn't like me at all," she said.

She knew there would be other movies, however; she would just have to hope they would be better ones. Meanwhile, her attention was being drawn away from Hollywood and the movies back to New York and the Broadway stage.

Fade Out—Fade In, a musical comedy about moviemaking in the 1930s, seemed the perfect show for Carol Burnett. It gave her the opportunity to sing and dance and clown, and to celebrate the movies she had so loved when she was growing up. But the show ran only a few months. At about the same time, "The Entertainers," a television variety show featuring Carol and produced by Joe, quietly ended its brief run.

This period might have been seen as a low point in Carol's life were it not for the birth of her daughter Carrie Louise in January 1964. Three years later, in

January 1967, a second daughter, Jody Ann, was born.

Carol loved being a mother, and she was having second thoughts about working long hours in the theater or movies. More and more, television looked good to her. "Television is the sanest, as far as the hours are concerned. When you work long hours," she said, "you become 'Aunt Mommy' to your children."

Once again, her life was changing direction. She was a mother. She was about to return to television. And she would soon be one of the most popular entertainers in America. Before that chapter in her life began, however, another chapter ended.

Late in 1967, her beloved Nanny died at the age of eighty-one. Carol had visited her at the nursing home where she spent her last months. Now she found herself seated next to her cousin Janice at the funeral. She smiled at the memories of jelly jars and movies, endless movies. She cried to remember the fights between Nanny and Mama. And then she thanked her lucky stars that when she was growing up, Nanny was always there for her—through the laughter and the tears, the thorns and the roses.

6

"The Carol Burnett Show"

"The Carol Burnett Show" went on the air September 11, 1967. It would run for eleven years, a total of 286 shows. Carol and her supporting players would perform in nearly 1,500 comedy sketches and 500 musical numbers by the time of the final broadcast, and it would rank as one of the most popular television programs of all time.

"I'm most comfortable when I'm playing to a live audience," Carol said, so every show was taped before an audience. The lights went up and Carol stepped down to the edge of the stage, inviting questions.

"Will you be singing any songs?" a man called out from the audience of her very first show.

"Yes, I will," Carol said, smiling. "Thanks for asking, Uncle Joe." Everyone laughed. Carol's joke implied that only a member of the family would ask to hear *her* voice, but the audience knew better. The man wasn't really Carol's Uncle Joe, and he, like everyone else, really wanted to hear her sing.

Over the years, Carol answered hundreds of questions, sometimes the same ones again and again. She signed autographs, willingly went along with requests for kisses, and encouraged young people who wanted show business careers. "It can happen to anybody," she'd say, laughing.

And the audience laughed with her, believing that if someone as normal and down-to-earth as Carol Burnett could become a star, anyone could.

Carol was comfortable with her studio audience. Her lighthearted banter made them feel comfortable, too. By the time she finished the question-and-answer session and told the audience at home, "Don't go away, we'll be right back," she had created a mood as relaxed and familiar as a family picnic.

Carol knew the value of a strong acting team because she had been part of the Garry Moore group. She had now put together her own team, one that would become the backbone (and funnybone) of her

show: Harvey Korman, Lyle Waggoner, Vicki Lawrence, and Tim Conway.

One of the comedy sketches on that first show—one that would become a regular feature for years—was based on her own life. In it, Carol and her TV husband, played by Harvey Korman, were seen raising Carol's younger sister. This provided the chance for lots of "teenager versus adults" joking. It provided an even greater chance for Vicki Lawrence, who really was a teenager.

As the younger sister, Vicki soon became one of Carol's television family, as did everyone else who worked on "The Carol Burnett Show." Carol's choreographer (the person who stages the dance numbers), said, "People get the impression that we're a family operation, and they're right."

Each "Carol Burnett Show" drew to a close in the same manner every week, much the way the very first one ended. Carol, dressed as a cleaning lady and carrying a mop, sat on an overturned bucket and sang a song. The song was a little sad, but before it was over, Carol's voice had turned strong and brassy. What started out as a cry of unhappiness became a cry of courage. After the final commercial break, she thanked her guest stars, asking each of them for their autograph to put in her scrapbook. Then she tugged her earlobe (a signal for her children, now that Nanny was gone),

and sang her closing number, "It's Time to Say So Long."

Waving good night to her audience in the studio and the millions of people watching at home, Carol was still smiling. She always looked as if she was having fun. And she was.

Soon she was the mother of three daughters. The third, Erin Kate, was born in August 1968. Carol now lived in a huge Hollywood mansion (with lots of closets!), located just minutes from the studio. And her work schedule was set up in a way that allowed her to spend plenty of time with the children.

She rarely left her house before noon each day, and she learned her music by listening to a tape recorder in her car on the way to work. Rehearsals lasted about five hours, Mondays through Thursdays. On Monday nights, she memorized her lines.

Friday's rehearsals brought in costumes, props, lighting—everything but the audience, who didn't arrive until four in the afternoon for the first taping. At seven-fifteen a second taping took place before a different audience. The director and producers chose the best from the two shows and edited them together.

It was a tiring week's work, but Carol and Joe (the show's executive producer) were home most nights for dinner. As important as the show was to them, their family came first.

Carol left the writing of the show to the writers, but they knew what it was she liked best. Poking fun at everything from TV commercials to supermarket checkout lines, she would do anything for a laugh. Yell like Tarzan. Fall down. Walk into a door. Black out her teeth. She got viewers to laugh at themselves by laughing at her.

But sometimes critics felt she went too far in playing for laughs. Two of her favorite targets of humor were the movies and the family. Her spoofs of the movies, from classics to then current hits, were gentle, affectionate, and often hysterically funny. When she looked at the family, she was just as funny but not nearly as gentle.

One of her mother's favorite sayings had been "Comedy is tragedy plus time." It was one Carol quoted often. This saying could have two meanings. One is that something can feel terrible when it happens, but seem harmless and even funny after enough time has passed. The other is that being funny is a way of dealing with your pain, but it is only possible after some time has gone by.

In Carol's comic families, husbands and wives were

always fighting, children screamed at their parents, parents resented their children. The young were misunderstood; the old were lonely. And happiness seemed just about impossible.

The character she liked best, and one that became a favorite of her audience as well, was named Eunice (say "YOU-nuss"). Eunice fought bitterly with her husband, Ed, but her greatest rage was saved for her mother, whom she called Mama.

"They had to lash out," Carol once said of her *real* mother and grandmother. "They didn't listen to each other. So many families don't. But they needed that relationship. That's what kept them alive."

Carol knew the truth behind her comedy. She had lived it. Her belief seemed to be: if we don't laugh, we'll have to cry. Even if her critics sometimes didn't understand that, her audiences did. And they agreed.

They also knew that, in real life, Carol Burnett wasn't a bitter drunk or a loud-mouthed screamer like the ones she sometimes portrayed. She wasn't a loser at all.

In 1977, a poll revealed that she was one of the world's twenty most admired women. And in other polls that year and the next two, she was voted the most popular all-around female entertainer.

But even when her life couldn't have seemed more fairy-tale perfect, she was changing. She needed once again to go in new directions, to challenge herself in new ways. And so on August 9, 1978, "The Carol Burnett Show" ended after eleven years. The audience gave Carol a standing ovation, a small but heartfelt "thank you" for all she had given them.

And she sang "It's Time to Say So Long."

7

Happily Ever After

Perhaps the greatest change in Carol over those eleven years was in the way she saw herself.

"In our question-and-answer sessions," she said, "I put down my face, I put down my figure. It got a big laugh, so for a long time I would do put-down jokes on myself. . . . It wasn't until the sixth or seventh year of our show that I started to realize I didn't have to do it, that I was a mature woman who could still be funny without crossing my eyes all the time."

Pete 'n' Tillie, Carol's second movie, was released in 1972. It would mark the beginning of a different Carol Burnett.

"Miss Burnett is the surprise," a critic wrote in the *New York Post.* "She is actress all the way, low key and sensitive—quite unlike the comedienne we usually see."

Carol herself wasn't entirely happy with her performance in *Pete 'n' Tillie.* But that performance laid the groundwork for others she would give in movies and television specials in the 1970s and 1980s.

In 1979, Carol played the part of a woman whose son was killed during the Vietnam War, not by the enemy, but accidentally by American forces. A television movie based on a true story, *Friendly Fire* wasn't the sort of thing people were used to seeing Carol do. But it was one of her greatest triumphs.

The part of Peg Mullen was a demanding one for the actress who played it. "No, it wasn't fun," Carol told an interviewer. "But it was fulfilling. What I like most about the woman I played can be found in one line of her dialogue: 'When it's your son, there's only one side.' "

That was a line that could have come from an episode in Carol's own life, one that undoubtedly added power and strength to her performance in *Friendly Fire.* Two years earlier, Carol had learned that her oldest daughter, Carrie, then thirteen, was hooked on drugs. Stunned by the discovery, she'd fought for her daughter's life like a mother tiger. Carrie was soon enrolled in a program to help her become drug-free.

All the while, Carol talked openly about the problem. She went public with this very private part of her life because she didn't want to hide from her fans. Even more important, she hoped she could help other families in trouble.

Though this was a time of terrible pain for Carol, it is typical that she didn't show her pain when she talked publicly. It is also typical that she gave Carrie all the credit for getting better. "We're so proud of what she's done for herself," she said. And it is perhaps that pride in Carrie's accomplishment that helped the teenager stay clear of drugs in the years to come.

Carol's personal problems didn't end there. The *National Enquirer,* a newspaper, falsely reported that she had been drunk and disorderly in a restaurant in 1976. Carol sued and finally won the case in 1981, but it took its toll on her energy and emotions.

Even after the case was settled, she said of it, "It will never, ever, not be a part of me." After all, her parents had died because of alcohol. To be accused of being drunk was, in her words, "disgusting" and "a pack of lies."

And then, in 1982, she and Joe divorced after nineteen years of marriage. Though she was reluctant to talk publicly about the breakup of her second marriage, the reason for it seems to be that, once again, Carol was changing. She had married an older man who did the talking and made the decisions for her. Now she was learning to speak out and make her own decisions. The time had come for her to go her own way.

There was something Carol *was* eager to talk about the year of her divorce, however. Another dream was coming true.

Carol's favorite kind of movie growing up had been the sort once advertised as "all-singing, all-dancing"— the movie musical. She had poked fun at these movies on her TV series, but she'd never had the chance to act in one herself. There was good reason: movie musicals were very expensive to make, and they weren't as popular with audiences as they had been when Carol was a child.

Then along came *Annie.*

Based on the popular sixty-year-old cartoon strip "Little Orphan Annie," the musical play *Annie* was a tremendous hit. It was still running on Broadway when a Hollywood studio paid over 9 million dollars for the right to make it into a movie.

Carol was cast as Miss Hannigan, the cruel warden of the orphans at the Hudson Street Home for Girls. Miss Hannigan was so unsympathetic to her charges she was known to growl, "Why any kid would want to be an orphan is beyond me."

Theater audiences had loved the stage version of

Annie. But would people go to the movies to see an "all-singing, all-dancing" story of a "ten-year-old and a mutt," when for the same five dollars they could be hurtled into space or back in time?

Over 40 million dollars was spent to find out. And the sad answer at first seemed to be: No. Critics were not happy with *Annie,* mentioning over and over again the ways in which all those millions of dollars had been wasted.

Whatever the critics thought, however, audiences loved *Annie*—not enough to make it the financial success its makers would have liked, but enough to win it a place as one of those movies children loved to see again and again. Is there a child who doesn't know at least some of the words to its most popular song, "Tomorrow"?

As for Carol's portrayal of the hard-hearted Miss Hannigan, the critics and the audiences agreed. A reviewer for *New York* magazine wrote: "This is the best work Burnett has done in the movies."

Still, some critics found fault with her performance, just as they had once had a hard time with how she portrayed family life on her TV series. Why, they wanted to know, did she have to play Miss Hannigan as a drunk? It was not the first time in her career she'd been accused of playing drunk for laughs. Those writers who knew about her childhood wondered how she could be so insensitive to the tragedy of alcoholism.

"When I was doing the TV show," Carol said in response to this criticism, "I played comic drunks—like Eunice—in several of the sketches, but every one of them came out a loser. Eunice is quite pitiful, for example, and so is Hannigan. All alcoholics are losers."

"Comedy is tragedy plus time." Beneath the laughter, there is pain.

When *Annie* came out in 1982, Carol Burnett had been making America laugh for over twenty-five years. She had won many awards and received many honors. In response to the condition of her thousand-dollar loan that she help others as she had been helped, she had established scholarships and given generously to many charities. And she had learned to speak out—against drugs and for the rights of women.

Carol had started out pretending to be other people. And in the process she had discovered it was all right to be herself. She once believed she was ugly, but found that every person is beautiful in her or his own way.

"You can't ever take anyone's place," she once said. "But no one in the world can take your place either. There's always a place for you."

Once upon a time there lived a skinny little girl with straight brown hair and scratched-up knees. She wondered what her place in the world would be. And then one day she found it.

"As long as they keep laughing," said Carol Burnett, "I'll live happily ever after."

ABOUT THIS BOOK

I can remember the day my family got its first television set. It was during the 1950s, when I was eight or nine, and television was something new and exciting. There were many wonderful comedians performing on TV then, but Carol Burnett made me laugh harder than just about anybody. I was a sucker for her fall-down, walk-into-walls, cross-the-eyes, and stick-out-the-tongue kind of humor.

When I was asked to write this book, I spent many hours at the Library of the Performing Arts in New York City. There I found file folders filled with articles going back to the beginning of Carol's career. I was helped, too, by watching reruns of her TV series, which was on the air in a shortened version called "Carol Burnett and Friends." At the Museum of Broadcasting, also in New York, I watched the very first "Carol Burnett Show." And about the time I was finishing my research, her autobiography, *One More Time,* was published. I recommend it to older readers interested in learning more about her childhood and early career.

Carol Burnett did more for me than make me laugh, however. Watching her taught me how to make other people laugh. As a writer of humorous children's books and a former actor and theater director, I've put that lesson to use many times.

And as Carol might say (and I hope you would agree): There is nothing like the sound of laughter.

J.H.